12 IMMIGRANTS WHO MADE
AMERICAN
ENTERTAINMENT GREAT

by Brandon Terrell

12
STORY
LIBRARY

www.12StoryLibrary.com

12-Story Library is an imprint of Bookstaves.

Photographs ©: Axelle/Bauer-Griffin/FilmMagic/Getty Images, cover, 1; Library of Congress, 4; Jack Mitchell/CC4.0, 5; Featureflash Photo Agency/Shutterstock.com, 6; World Economic Forum/CC2.0, 7; Tinseltown/Shutterstock.com, 8; Khin Maung Win/Associated Press, 9; JStone/Shutterstock.com, 10; Philippe Wojazer/Pool/Abaca/Sipa USA/Associated Press, 11; Gage Skidmore/CC3.0, 12; Mustafa Quraishi/Associated Press, 13; Kathy Hutchins/ Shutterstock.com, 14; © Natalie Portman.com, 15; Sam Aronov/Shutterstock.com, 16; Disney/ABC Televison Group/CC2.0, 17; Tinseltown/Shutterstock.com, 18; Augie Rose/ Everett Collection/Alamy Stock Photo, 19; Kathy Hutchins/Shutterstock.com, 20; Jack Fordyce/Shutterstock.com, 21; DFree/Shutterstock.com, 22; Ms. magazine/CC4.0, 23; Featureflash Photo Agency/Shutterstock.com, 24; Featureflash Photo Agency/Shutterstock. com, 25; Tinseltown/Shutterstock.com, 26; WEBN-TV/CC2.0, 27; PD, 28; Nickolas Murray/ PD, 29

ISBN
978-1-63235-573-7 (hardcover)
978-1-63235-627-7 (paperback)
978-1-63235-688-8 (ebook)

Library of Congress Control Number: 2018943228

Printed in the United States of America
Mankato, MN
June 2018

About the Cover
Lupita Nyong'o in 2017.

Access free, up-to-date content on this topic plus a full digital version of this book. Scan the QR code on page 31 or use your school's login at 12StoryLibrary.com.

Table of Contents

John Lennon Changes Rock Music

On February 9, 1964, the British band the Beatles appeared on American TV. They played five songs on *The Ed Sullivan Show*. They changed rock music forever. John Lennon started the band that became the Beatles.

Lennon was born on October 9, 1940, in Liverpool, a city in England. In 1956, he formed a band called the Quarrymen. He met Paul McCartney in 1957 and invited him to join the band. Lennon came up with the name the Beatles.

The Beatles recorded their first single, "Love Me Do," in 1962. In 1964, they made their first visit to the United States. Fans acted so crazy a new word was invented: Beatlemania. The Beatles made many albums. They starred in three movies. They played concerts all over the world.

Lennon quit the Beatles in 1969. He and his wife, artist Yoko Ono, moved to the United States in 1971. They spoke out against the Vietnam War. President Richard Nixon wanted

to deport them. When Nixon resigned, Lennon was granted permanent US residency.

Lennon continued to sing and write songs. One of his songs, "Imagine," became a famous antiwar anthem.

Lennon died on December 8, 1980. He was shot and killed by a man named Mark David Chapman. Many people believe that Lennon's music will live forever.

STRAWBERRY FIELDS FOREVER

John Lennon and Yoko Ono lived near Central Park in New York City. Five years after Lennon died, a memorial in the park was dedicated to him. It's a special Quiet Zone in the park. People go there to think and remember John. There is a mosaic with the word "Imagine" at its center.

600 million

Number of Beatles' albums sold worldwide.

- John Lennon and Paul McCartney met in 1957.
- The Beatles first appeared on American TV on February 9, 1964.
- Lennon kept making music until his death in 1980.

Charlize Theron Lights Up the Big Screen

Charlize Theron is a successful actress and film producer. She was born on August 7, 1975, in Benoni, South Africa. Her parents owned a farm and ran a road construction company. Her first language was Afrikaans. At age six, Theron started taking ballet lessons. At 18, she won a scholarship to the Joffrey Ballet School in New York City. She wanted to be a ballet dancer. But a knee injury meant she could never have a career in dance.

Theron decided to try acting. She moved to Hollywood in California. She soon discovered that her South African accent made it hard to get acting roles. She learned to speak with an American accent.

She began with small parts. Bigger parts followed. In 2003, she starred in a movie called *Monster*. She won the Academy Award for Best Actress. Theron has starred in many movies since then.

She also helps people in need. In 2007, she started the Charlize

7.1 million

People living with HIV in South Africa in 2016.

- Charlize Theron wanted to be a ballet dancer.
- She won a Best Actress Oscar in 2004 for the movie *Monster*.
- Theron is a UN Messenger of Peace.

THINK ABOUT IT

Do you help people in your community? What do you do to help? Are there other ways you would like to help? How can you get started?

Theron Africa Outreach Project (CTAOP). The project helps keep youth in South Africa safe from diseases like HIV/AIDS. A mobile health clinic visits high schools in rural communities. Because of her work with CTAOP, the United Nations named Theron a UN Messenger of Peace.

Theron became a United States citizen in 2008. She also kept her South African citizenship. She is a citizen of both nations.

Jackie Chan Mixes Martial Arts with Humor

Jackie Chan has made more than 200 movies. He has broken many bones. He was a big star in Asia before he was famous in the United States.

Chan was born in Hong Kong on April 7, 1954. His parents were not wealthy. When Chan was a child, he and his father would wake up early to practice kung fu.

From age seven, Chan attended the China Drama Academy. He studied acting, acrobatics, and martial arts. After graduating in 1971, he worked as a stunt man. One of his early movies was *Fist of Fury*. The star was kung fu legend Bruce Lee. When Lee died in 1973, some people called Chan the next star of Hong Kong cinema. But Chan didn't want to be like Lee. He wanted to be himself. He started mixing martial arts with humor. He did his own stunts, and he made people laugh.

Before long, Chan was the highest-paid actor in Hong Kong. In 1998, he starred in the American comedy *Rush Hour*. It was a hit. Many more films followed. In 2016, Chan received an honorary Academy Award.

Offscreen, Chan supports many causes. These include animal rights, disaster relief, and wildlife conservation. In 2004, Chan became a UNICEF Goodwill Ambassador. UNICEF is the United Nations International Children's Emergency Fund.

TWO WORLD RECORDS

Jackie Chan is a two-time Guinness World Record holder. He holds the world records for Most Credits in One Movie and Most Stunts by a Living Actor. Chan has risked his life many times as a stunt man. The world records recognize his life's work.

62

Jackie Chan's age when he won his honorary Oscar.

- As a child, Jackie Chan practiced kung fu with his father.
- Chan does all of his own stunts.
- He developed his own style of mixing martial arts with humor.

Rihanna Is a Global Sensation

$75 million
Rihanna's earnings in 2016.

- Rihanna grew up in Barbados.
- She became a global sensation after the release of her song "Umbrella."
- She started a charity called the Clara Lionel Foundation.

Rihanna is an international pop star and fashion icon. She was born on February 20, 1988, on the Caribbean island of Barbados. She is the oldest of three children. Her full name is Robyn Rihanna Fenty. As a child, she struggled with headaches. Her home life wasn't happy. When Rihanna was 14, her parents divorced.

Rihanna began singing at an early age. Some of her influences were Madonna, Janet Jackson, and Mariah Carey. In 2003, when Rihanna was 15, she started a music group with two friends. They performed for a New York music producer who was visiting Barbados. A year later, Rihanna moved to Connecticut to make a demo album. In 2005, she auditioned for Def Jam Records and its president, the rapper Jay-Z. Rihanna was very nervous, but she grew confident when she sang. Later that year, her first album, *Music of the Sun*, reached number 10 on the Billboard albums chart.

In 2007, Rihanna's third album, *Good Girl Gone Bad*, came out. She became a worldwide sensation. Her song "Umbrella," featuring Jay-Z, topped the Billboard chart for 52 weeks. It earned a Grammy Award for Best Rap/Song Collaboration. As of 2018, Rihanna has won nine Grammys. She is also acting in TV shows and movies.

Rihanna's talents go beyond entertainment. She designs clothes. She worked with a makeup company to help women and children affected by HIV/AIDS. In 2012, she founded the Clara Lionel Foundation, named for her grandparents. The foundation works to improve health and education in communities around the world.

Rihanna speaks at the Global Partnership for Education Conference in Dakar, Senegal, in 2018.

M. Night Shyamalan Makes Movies with a Twist

It seems everyone knows the phrase "I see dead people." These words were whispered by a little boy in the movie *The Sixth Sense*. This was the movie that made director M. Night Shyamalan famous.

Shyamalan was born on August 6, 1970, in Puducherry, India. His parents were doctors. Soon after, the family immigrated to the United States. They settled in Pennsylvania.

When Shyamalan was eight years old, he was given a Super 8 film camera. He made 45 short films by the time he was 15. His father wanted him to be a doctor. His mother told him to follow his passion.

Shyamalan went to film school at New York University. He completed his first feature film before he graduated in 1993. *The Sixth Sense* was his third feature film. It came out in 1999 and became a big hit. It was nominated for six Academy Awards including Best Picture and Best Director.

Shyamalan pushes the boundaries of storytelling. He likes to add shocking endings and twists. Films like

Unbreakable, Signs, and *The Village* gave audiences scares and shivers. One of Shyamalan's favorite twists is to play a small role in his own movies. He learned this from the director Alfred Hitchcock.

In 2008, the president of India gave Shyamalan the Padma Shri award. It goes to people who have made significant achievements in their fields.

15

Number of films M. Night Shyamalan has directed, as of 2018.

- Shyamalan was born in India but grew up in Pennsylvania.
- He studied film at New York University.
- *The Sixth Sense* was the third film he directed, and his first big hit.

THINK ABOUT IT

What are some stories or movies you know that end with a twist? What makes this so surprising? Do you like twist endings? Why or why not?

Natalie Portman Is Hollywood Royalty

Natalie Portman has been acting in movies for most of her life. But she also knows it's important to get a good education.

She was born in Jerusalem on June 9, 1981. Her father is Israeli. Her mother is American. Three years later, the family immigrated to the United States. They settled in Long Island, New York. When Portman was nine, she was discovered at a pizza parlor. A scout for a makeup company asked if she wanted to be a model. She said she wanted to act.

Starting in 1994, she played several small movie roles. Her big break came when George Lucas made her a queen. Lucas created the *Star Wars* franchise. He was about to make three more *Star Wars* films. He cast Portman as Padmé Amidala, Queen of Naboo.

Portman became an international star. But even with a successful film career, she focused on her education. She graduated from Harvard University in 2003. In 2011, she won a Best Actress Academy Award for the movie *Black Swan*.

Portman supports many charities. One of them is WE Charity, which helps families lift themselves out of poverty. In 2015, Portman visited Kenya to help build a girls' school.

$2.5 billion

Worldwide box office earnings for the three *Star Wars* prequels.

- Natalie Portman was born in Israel.
- At age nine, she was discovered by a scout for a makeup company.
- Portman starred in the *Star Wars* prequels.

NO MEAT OR DAIRY

Natalie Portman is a vegan. She doesn't eat or use animal products. Portman was a vegetarian for years. She switched to being vegan because she loves animals. She wants a cruelty-free lifestyle. She believes that factory farming is bad for the environment and for people. She also chooses to avoid the fat, calories, and salt in processed food.

7

Trevor Noah Brings a Global View to American TV

Each weeknight on TV, Trevor Noah gives Americans his view of the day's news. He has his own show on Comedy Central. It's called *The Daily Show with Trevor Noah*. He has come a long way from his beginnings.

Noah was born on February 20, 1984, in Soweto, South Africa. His mother is black. His father is white. At the time, South Africa was under apartheid. This is a strict system of racial segregation.

It was illegal for black people and white people to have children together. Noah was proof that a crime had been committed.

Noah was raised by his mother and grandmother. They were poor and often hungry. But his mother, Patricia, was brave and wise. She spoke several languages, and she taught Noah. He learned from her to face injustice with humor.

Apartheid ended in 1991. As a teenager, Noah acted in a TV soap opera. Then a friend dared him to try stand-up comedy. Noah became one of the most famous comedians in South Africa. In 2011, he moved to the United States. Noah appeared on *The Tonight Show with Jay Leno* in 2012. In 2014, he got a job with *The Daily Show with Jon Stewart*.

Stewart retired from the show in 2015. Noah became the new host. *The Daily Show with Trevor Noah* first aired on September 28, 2015. The show is very popular. One reason is because Noah sees things differently. He takes a global view.

Noah is only 34 years old, but he has already written a book about his life. It is called *Born a Crime*. Noah wrote it as a love letter for his mother.

6

Number of languages Trevor Noah speaks.

- Noah was born in Soweto, South Africa.
- He grew up under apartheid, a system of racial discrimination.
- Noah became the host of *The Daily Show* in 2015.

Salma Hayek Breaks Barriers

Salma Hayek is one of the first Latina actresses to find success in the United States. She was born in Veracruz, Mexico, on September 2, 1966. When she was 12, her parents sent her to school in the United States. Later she acted in soap operas on Mexican TV. She became a big star in her home country. But when she moved to Los Angeles in 1991, she found there were almost no parts for Latina women. Hayek had to start over as an actress.

She worked hard on her English and her acting. Director Robert Rodriguez cast her in a 1995 film called *Desperado.* That made it easier for Hayek to get more movie roles.

Hayek had a dream role in mind. She wanted to play the Mexican artist Frida Kahlo. She produced and starred in the film called *Frida.* It came out in 2002. *Frida* received six Academy Award nominations. One was for best actress. Hayek was the first Mexican actress to get that nomination.

Since *Frida*, Hayek has starred in many movies. She has also worked in TV. But she wanted to do more than act and produce. In 2013, Hayek and Beyoncé cofounded

Chime for Change with the Gucci fashion company. This organization works for women's rights around the world. In 2018, Hayek won UNICEF's Danny Kaye Humanitarian Award for helping children.

8
Years it took Hayek to make *Frida*.

- Salma Hayek was born in Mexico.
- She was the first Mexican actress to be nominated for a Best Actress Oscar.
- Hayek cofounded Chime for Change with Beyoncé and Gucci.

CHIME FOR CHANGE

Because of Chime for Change, homeless women are going back to work. Young women in Nepal are rebuilding their communities after an earthquake. Girls in India and Tanzania are going to school. The organization has funded hundreds of projects. Many more are under way.

Justin Bieber Conquers Pop

When Justin Bieber was 12, he won second place in a talent contest. He posted videos on YouTube of himself singing. At first, he had hundreds of views, then thousands. A talent manager saw the videos. He helped Bieber get a record deal. Bieber's first single, "One Time," came out in 2009. It sold millions of copies.

Bieber was born on March 1, 1994, in London, Ontario, Canada. He was the only child of a single mother, Pattie Mallette. She encouraged his love for music. Bieber started playing drums when he was two years old. He taught himself to play piano, guitar, and trumpet.

After "One Time," Bieber made an EP with seven songs. The song "Baby" was his breakout hit. It sold 10 million digital copies. His 2011 movie *Justin Bieber: Never Say Never* became the #1 concert film of all time.

Ever since, Bieber's albums have sold millions of copies. His concert

50+

Number of Justin Bieber's tattoos.

- Justin Bieber started out as a YouTube sensation.
- His breakout hit, "Baby," sold 10 million digital copies.
- He is one of the highest-paid celebrities in the world.

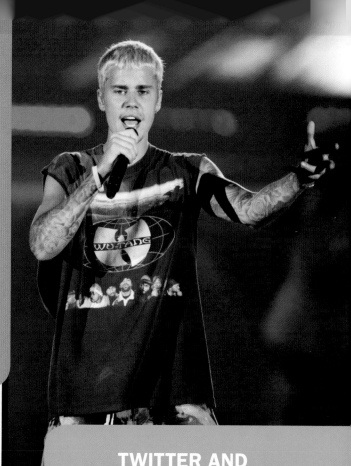

tours earn many millions of dollars. He has 99 million Instagram followers. In 2016, he became the first artist to reach 10 billion video views on Vevo, a video hosting service. He is one of the world's highest-paid celebrities.

Bieber has sometimes made headlines for bad behavior. In 2017, China banned him from performing in Beijing, its capital city. But his fans, called Beliebers, stick by him no matter what.

TWITTER AND CELEBRITIES

Celebrities use Twitter to communicate with fans, share news about their work, and improve their image. In 2017, Justin Bieber became the second person to reach 100 million Twitter followers. Katy Perry was first. In 2018, Perry and Bieber were still the top two most followed Twitter accounts. Former US president Barack Obama was third.

Lupita Nyong'o Speaks Out for Immigrants

Lupita Nyong'o is an Oscar-winning actress. She is also a voice for immigrants. Born on March 1, 1983, in Mexico City, Nyong'o was the second of six children. Her parents were political refugees from Kenya in Africa. Soon after Nyong'o was born, her family moved back to Kenya.

Nyong'o went to college in the United States. She graduated with a degree in film. She returned home to Kenya for the summer. A Hollywood movie was being filmed there. She got a job as a production assistant. But she wanted to be an actress.

Meanwhile she learned about directing and producing. In 2009, she edited a documentary film called *In My Genes*. She acted in a popular TV series. She went back to the United States for more education. In 2012, she received a master's degree from the Yale School of Drama.

Just before graduating, Nyong'o won a part in a film called *12 Years a Slave*. It is about slavery in the United States before the Civil War. This was her big Hollywood break.

The film won a Golden Globe award. Nyong'o won the Academy Award for Best Supporting Actress.

Nyong'o's star in Hollywood is on the rise. She has appeared in many films including *Star Wars Episode VII: The Force Awakens* and *Black Panther.* In June 2016, Nyong'o stood with other Hollywood stars to share their stories about being immigrants. They made a video about why immigrants are important to America's history and culture.

1000
Number of actresses who auditioned for Nyong'o's role in *12 Years a Slave.*

- Lupita Nyong'o was born in Mexico City when her parents were refugees.
- She grew up in Kenya.
- She won an Academy Award for her role in *12 Years a Slave.*

Ang Lee Makes His Mark on Hollywood

Ang Lee has won two Academy Awards for Best Director. He is someone who can work on many kinds of films. He can make a Western or a movie about ancient China. He can make a drama or a comedy. He can make a martial arts film or a superhero movie. Every film he works on is different.

Lee was born on October 23, 1954, in Taipei, Taiwan. He studied at the Taiwan Academy of Art. He decided he wanted to work on movies. His strict parents were against it. In 1979, he moved to the United States. He was shy, and it was hard to leave home. He studied theater in Illinois and film in New York.

Lee directed his first film in 1992. All three of his next films were nominated for Academy Awards. In 2001, *Crouching Tiger, Hidden Dragon* won four Academy Awards. His next film was *Hulk*, about the big green superhero.

For his next film, *Brokeback Mountain*, Lee won the Academy Award for Best Director. He was the first Asian to receive that award. Six years later, he won again for *Life of Pi*. This film tells the story

of a boy trapped at sea with a tiger. The movie relied on many special effects. It also won awards for those.

Ang Lee has been a director for many years. It is his work, not his ego, that makes him special.

700+
Number of visual effects shots in *Life of Pi*.

- Ang Lee grew up in Taiwan.
- He went to college for theater and film.
- He was the first Asian to win an Academy Award for Best Director.

THINK ABOUT IT

Several of Ang Lee's films have been adapted from books. Which of your favorite books would you turn into a movie?

Sofía Vergara Is a Powerful Woman

$41.5 million

Sofia Vergara's earnings in 2017.

- Sofia Vergara was born in Colombia.
- When she was 17, she was discovered by a photographer.
- She is one of the top-earning actresses on TV.

Sofía Vergara planned to be a dentist. But when she was 17, she took a walk on a beach. She was discovered by a photographer. Her first job was in a Pepsi commercial that aired in Latin America. Today she is the highest-paid TV actress in the world.

Vergara was born in Barranquilla, Colombia, on July 10, 1972. She was one of six children. Their father was a cattle rancher. Their mother was a homemaker. Vergara learned English at a bilingual elementary school. She worked as a model and hosted Colombian TV shows. In 1994, she moved to Miami. She hosted a TV show that aired on Univision. This is the United States' Spanish-language network.

Then came hard times in Vergara's life. In 1998, her older brother,

Rafael, was murdered in Colombia. In 2000, Vergara was diagnosed with cancer. The cancer treatment was successful. Vergara moved on with her career.

She starred in the film *Big Trouble*. She made guest appearances on TV shows. She acted in a Broadway play. She won a role in a new TV series called *Modern Family*. This show was an instant hit. Fans and critics loved it. Vergara played the role of Gloria Delgado-Pritchett. She and the rest of the cast became stars overnight. *Modern Family* was nominated for dozens of Emmy awards. It won more than 20 times. Vergara received four Emmy nominations.

Vergara's wealth isn't just from her *Modern Family* job. She has her own line of perfumes. She has a clothing line and a furniture line. She still works with Pepsi. She's a smart businesswoman.

Vergara became a US citizen in 2014. She got a perfect score on her citizenship test.

More Immigrants in History

Alfred Hitchcock

Alfred Hitchcock was born in London, England on August 13, 1899. He came to America in 1939. He directed more than 50 films including *Rear Window, Vertigo,* and *Psycho.* He was nicknamed the "Master of Suspense." Alfred Hitchcock died in 1980 at the age of 81.

Audrey Hepburn

Born in Belgium on May 4, 1929, Audrey Hepburn was one of Hollywood's greatest style icons. The successful actress starred in such films as *Roman Holiday* and *Breakfast at Tiffany's.* Hepburn is one of the few actresses to win an Academy Award, an Emmy, a Tony, and a Grammy. She died in 1993.

The Warner Brothers

The Warner Brothers were Albert, Sam, Harry, and Jack Warner. They were born in Poland and moved to Ohio in 1895. In 1903, they traveled around showing movies in tents. Four years later, they began producing movies. They started a movie production company in 1918. Today the Warner Brothers library includes 7,500 feature films and 4,500 television programs.

Elizabeth Taylor

Elizabeth Taylor was born in London, England, in 1932. She became a star in 1944 for her work on the film *National Velvet*. She was 12 years old. Taylor would go on to win Best Actress Academy Awards for *Butterfield 8* and *Who's Afraid of Virginia Woolf?* She was also known for her violet eyes. She died in 2011.

Elizabeth Taylor on the cover of *Modern Screen* in 1950.

Editor's note:
America is a nation of immigrants. This series celebrates important contributions immigrants have made to entertainment. In choosing the people to feature in this book, the author and 12-Story Library editors considered diversity of all kinds and the significance and stature of the work.

Glossary

achievement
Something that has been accomplished by ability, special effort, or courage.

charity
A fund, foundation, or institution dedicated to a particular cause.

citizenship
The state of having the rights, privileges, and duties of a citizen.

demo
Demo is short for demonstration. A demo recording is a song or group of songs made to show an artist's abilities and ideas.

deport
To expel an alien or unwanted person from a country.

EP
An extended play record. An EP has more songs than a single but isn't a full-length album.

humanitarian
Having concern for other people and helping to improve their lives.

immigrant
A person who has come to live in a country from another country or region. Some immigrants are refugees. Some ask for political asylum.

mosaic
A picture or design made from small pieces of glass, stone, or tiles.

nominated
Having been proposed for an honor or award.

refugee
A person who flees, especially to a foreign country, for safety and refuge.

For More Information

Books

Curtis, Jamie Lee. *This is Me: A Story of Who We Are and Where We Came From.* New York: Workman Publishing Group, 2016.

Benoit, Peter. *Immigration.* Cornerstones of Freedom: Bringing History to Life. Danbury, CT: Scholastic Library Publishing, 2012.

Visit 12StoryLibrary.com

Scan the code or use your school's login at **12StoryLibrary.com** for recent updates about this topic and a full digital version of this book. Enjoy free access to:

- Digital ebook
- Breaking news updates
- Live content feeds
- Videos, interactive maps, and graphics
- Additional web resources

Note to educators: Visit 12StoryLibrary.com/register to sign up for free premium website access. Enjoy live content plus a full digital version of every 12-Story Library book you own for every student at your school.

Index

About the Author

Brandon Terrell is a writer based in St. Paul, Minnesota. He is the author of numerous children's books including picture books, chapter books, and graphic novels. When not hunched over his laptop, Brandon enjoys watching movies and television, reading, baseball, and spending every spare moment with his wife and their two children.

READ MORE FROM 12-STORY LIBRARY

Every 12–Story Library Book is available in many fomats. For more information, visit 12StoryLibrary.com